SONGS FOR MY MOTHER

By Stephanie Jeannot

Stephanie Jeannot

SONGS FOR MY MOTHER

By Stephanie Jeannot

Stephanie Jeannot

Table of Contents

Dedicated to the strongest person I have ever met in my entire life who gave me so much of her love and time and never questioning sharing who she was with me. I call her mom. Thank you mom.

Stephanie Jeannot

Superwoman

She is always modeling love

and imparting life lessons to me.

I admire her Sage guidance

And how she wholeheartedly built her tight knit family

She makes me think expansively about life

To help me ward off any impending catastrophes

I only hope to someday be able to sip from her deep well of confidence.

Because with her examples, I'm fully equipped me to succeed.

My mother is a woven tapestry of truth

She always has love bubbling to the surface

She is one of the strongest people I know

Because she never doubts in her prowess

Overflowing with intelligence and care

With unlimited time to tend to our needs

Some might call her superwoman

But I call her mommy

Lessons for Days Ahead

With her quiet dignified strength

And the look of supreme confidence on her face

She tried in every way to elevate my mind

and to remove me of my ignorance

She would share her opinions when I didn't ask

Just to show that she had concerns about me

Even when I thought her budding in was annoying

she knew just how to send waves of joy through me

Like for instance in the way I dressed

Some would say was like a grandmother

She would make this face and it amped me to

Go back to my closet to change into another

And when I cooked and didn't follow recipes

She'd laugh and make the bad outcome seem okay

I've been so blessed to receive the love and guidance that she gave

Stephanie Jeannot

Hand-crafted So Wonderfully Complex

She was hand-crafted so wonderfully complex

She could finagle just about anything

One minute she is on a ladder painting walls

The next she is making a dress for a wedding

She has more might than a lion

She is a queen that sits crowned on a throne

Protecting her kingdom from plagues to their wellbeing

And sharing an overflowing stream of compassion

A regal woman capable of so many things

My mother, the jack of all trades

Humming and smiling all through the day

Despite my attempt to leapfrog ahead prematurely

And then giving me a dowry of great wisdom

To acknowledge and apply to life

Letting me know that she was a disciplinarian

And that I was under her watchful eyes

Like Father Like Daughter

She is like her dad who knew God really well

She was up early in the morning praising the Lord

Every day he would make his way to church service

And invite folks who might be interested in tagging along

He'd start every family function with a prayer for his people

Asking God to protect them from the pestilence

And my mom when she rises on the wings of the dawn

She shines the light or God because she knows she is blessed

The Hairstylist

I sat between her knees at night as she braided my hair

Telling me stories and making me laugh without a care

As she added grease to my scalp and carefully parted the strands

She has always been so very diligent with her hands

Passing the comb through the naps gently so it would not hurt

And moisturizing the cry kinks that were dying of thirst

The Erudite

Whenever I saw her walking with her heels

And strutting like a supermodel

I thought to myself I want to be like her

A royal queen that truly sparkles

Rising up early for work and coming home to tend to us

Cooking up deliciousness from scratch without a fuss

And then helping us with our homework to make sure we did it right

Show us that she was both physically strong and an erudite

Mother May I

It was almost like the game Mother may I

If you asked and your request was denied

If you dared to move to do what she protected you from anyway

You might have to be on your knees all day

But if she said yes you could do the very thing

You found joy in her response and would move along smiling

Ayitien Kulture

Rice and beans and beans and rice

And sugar makes ti belle fee look nice

And mais moulin and greo

And water to make her little flowers grow

And legume and pom de tere

And songs of Bondye's mercies being flung in the air

And culture of the Haitian sounds

Tabou Combo and System band

To Kompa dance and drink cremas

And speak in Haitian tongues and bay blag

While playing dominoes on the side

And eating bunun peze that's fried

And hearing decabez while we dancee

Enjoy some of the many Haitian mores

Traditions shared before our eyes

To keep our Haitian culture alive

Beautiful Tresses

Some people cry when they see grey hair

It makes them consider themselves as old

At least that is the way that things were

Until now when it seems like silver hair is like gold

The Bible says that it is a sign of righteousness

So, for me seeing grey made me happy

Not that I am dying to grow old

But then it must mean that there's some good in me

And seeing my mom's beautiful tresses

All shiny and silver and soft

And it made me think that maybe mine will be that way

When my youthful days come to a halt

Because grey hair is not so bad if you think about it

So many experiences you've seen and can share

I'd only be lucky to have something

As beautiful as my mother's hair

Baking Ingredients

I always saw my mom making cakes

For everybody for every special occasion

As beautiful as a golden star

Hovering over the nation

And so, I thought maybe I inherited that skill

Of being a great baker

Which made me gather up the ingredients

to beat, mix and created into cake batter

Of course, I'm not as skilled at following recipes

She follows word for word the recipes and makes masterpieces

I on the other hand follow for a bit and do my own thing

And then I pull the platter out the oven and its broken in pieces

If only I had been as diligent and patient as she is

If only I followed the recipes to make a good cake

And that is when I realize I may neither cook as good as her

Nor will I be as skilled as she is to bake

Triumphant Leader

A mother is a triumphant leader of men and women

She leads the pack, and everyone follows her

because she always shows strength in her stride.

She always shows an air of command.

She is always diligently working,

Always busy in her manual toils with her family on her mind

And always doing something that benefits those around.

She claims the mantle of power just being who she is

A person who truly impacts lives

Song Bursts

Where two or three are gathered is said to be like church

And I was taught about God from the day of my birth

Walking to St Rose to sing in the church choir

Or hearing of God's mercies with my mom's song bursts

Back in the Days

With a few of the neighborhood kids

I remember playing in the yard on the swings

Or playing hopscotch, tag or double-dutch

My life was filled to the brim with so much love

My friends used to refer to our yard as the playground

And then I'd hear my mother call my name out loud

It's time to come inside she'd say

After the whole day we played

And ran from the bulldog on our block

And then the clock said six 0'clock

It was time for dinner with the family at the table

Back then we didn't have cellphones or cable

No Facebook or IG or teleconferencing while eating

We couldn't ignore each other because we were texting

We had good times and it was always a treat

Just thinking about those good old days makes me feel so free

Stephanie Jeannot

How Did She Know

You would think she had boundless energy always busy doing something

She was always aware as if she had eyes in the back of her head

As if there was a chip in my body to hear everything I said

Bread Soup

Tomatoes and bread and water added

To heal me from my infirmities

A little bit of spaghetti to spice it up

My momma's read soup always brought healing for me

Ready For the World

She sent me pealing along with strength and knowledge

Teaching me about the world at my fingertips

Though she had t take my rudeness to show me about life

Thinking I was ready for the world before time would even permit

Hero is Her Name

Our mother who art the head of our household

Hero is her name

Her household held down because she wore the crown

and was regal in how she handled things

She faced each day with good heart and emotion

And forgave us even when she had to voice her disapproval for our ignorance

And she passed on her strong faith to her children

While maintaining calm in her house

Or even while easing on down the road in her station wagon

Fulfilling responsibilities of work, family and home

Sharing

She had one foot in America and one foot in Haiti

And was so proud to share her country with her babies

Speaking in Kreyol and cooking Haitian Cuisine in the kitchen

And sharing her experiences when we weren't too hardheaded to listen

Footprints

Whenever we were making big strides she was there

She showed us how to love and how to care

She told us education was very important

And when we didn't know the answers she helped us solve it

She stood there with a smile

As we waked to get our diplomas

Or while we were on stage in school plays taking on different personas

Or when we needed an ear to listen

While we talked away

And even when we didn't want to be along and wanted to just pray

In Her Wings

Was it hearing her singing through the house that made me love it

I was on the verge of womanhood standing in her wings

Watching her showcase her gentleness that I only wished to have

She always shared a heart of abundance without any strings attached

Examples

If she were a song

It would be a love song with a catchy hook

If she were story

It would be featured in the most interesting book

Andi f she were an art piece

It would be a genuine masterpiece with vibrant colors

Like a long overdue breeze

In a heatwave during the summer

Yes She Is

A mother is a philosopher extraordinaire

She is the first teacher you'll ever know

She is the waters of nature that fall on the land

That help the buds of hyacinth flowers grow

The busiest of bees that is always working and giving her best

To nourish her children with love and catapult them to greatness

Her Advice Proved to Be Right

If someone tells you that life is easy, they are telling you half-truths. Listen to your mother when she is trying to tell you the right things to do. I didn't realize at the time that I was learning from someone who already walked the path. Part of the exasperating work of being a disciplinarian involves listening to angry responses from her kids talking back.

I was heavily melded to the idea of being older because I had a limited appetite for life. I wanted to fly off into the sky like an eagle above the sky. I never realized that being under the lash of being older would be so demanding. I thought that I would be merrily on my way into independently standing.

I thought having my big moment would be much different than a powerful environment for pedagogical purposes. I did not know that being older meant dealing first-hand with life's unpredictable twists and turns. I had no idea that one should not advance in their stead before it is actually their due time. I had no idea that I had been imperiling my own life. And now I realize that her advice proved to be right.

I never realized that she was trying to prepare me for the world to come. Instead, I would respond in frantic outbursts because I was too hardheaded to listen. Sometimes I feel overwhelmed with sorrow for not giving more thought to how I was responding to her generous instruction. Instead, I went wandering without regard to the words for success she was providing.

She had no problems sharing things like the wisdom she tried to impart. If I had any advice to share that you might want to apply to your heart, it is to not allow toxic habits to overpower the wealth of information she teaches. I would say to listen to your mother and all of her many valuable speeches.

You will then realize the confidence she has in you and how much she truly is rooting you on. Her strength and wisdom are just some of the many features that fall under the umbrella of the person you call mom.

She transcends all clichés. She is the bravest of the brave. She has a soft heart when being your cheerleader at parades. She adjusts her crown as a queen and how can I not fully beam at how she exemplifies herself as a true leader which is why you always seem to need her.

She is the commander of the ship she calls home and within who you are, she is your backbone. A wonderful sketch like a museum display. She is the solved puzzle of a sudoku game. She is a singer in her heart always with a song of joy. She developed a steady environment for her troop of girls and boys. She is always working and always busting her butt for countless hours in her day. And every Sunday she is at the church chapel on the kneeler as she prays.

She has the most beautiful glow on her face. Her culture she shares for us to embrace. And giving us sound advice to apply. She never failed to put in her effort and time. Even while driving her station wagon on the 95, she would share stories with us on how to rise. No one can compare to a mother in your life because God hand crafted her so unique that she is one of a kind.

She Put Her Foot In It

Anybody who has experience making meals in the kitchen knows that it requires a lot of effort to make; especially if you are cooking for your family. And so, part of the process of getting prepared to cook is to put your whole mind and heart into it.

I would like to set the record straight; my mother is the best cook on the planet.

Even though my mom worked hard all day, she was always ready to put her foot into the food that she was making. I complimented her on one of her meals once and told her that she put her foot in it and she said, "I put my feet in it." Who wouldn't be humored by her incomprehension of my slang? But when I say that she put her foot into the things that she would concoct in the kitchen, there is no half-truth being told here.

My mother knew exactly what to do to make real change to the way that cries of our hunger pangs. Purpose bubbled to the surface with every action she made in creating her meals.

She had a way to put a unique spin on everything and to do anything she put her hands on with greatness. She had more food preparation tools in her arsenal than Home Depot on any given day and made the extra effort to add a flowing spring of heart, mind, spirit and soul. She knew how to deliver smiles easily.

I saw her take scotch bonnet peppers, onions, garlic and parsley to make her own blend of spice to put on food while on the oven cooking. I also envied her for that. I was the more, store bought in a bottle spice type of chef but my mom, she would use all-natural products and create her own concoctions and the end result was always so good.

She would get into the kitchen and slave away for hours while letting a tune go out of her heart.

"Amazing grace, how sweet the sound."

She would sing and clean the meats with lemon and vinegar.

"That saved a wretch like me!"

She would hum and stir the beans on the way to achieving tender consistency and then I would feel the joys of her singing and join into the musical celebration.

"I once was lost but now am found."

She would echo sounds as she added water to a pot and added olive oil to boil before adding rice.

"T 'was blind but now I see!"

The song was blaring through the whole house while the aromas were spilling out from the kitchen, right into our noses.

We were always so anxious to take a peek to see exactly what was brewing and so every time my mom left the room, we crept in to take a look and also a pinch-full of whatever was in the pots.

I'm pretty sure she knew what we were doing when we were doing it but her regality would not allow her to be moved in her positive stance.

She kept singing, moving around the kitchen and she just continued laboring along to get her custom-made meal prepared.

I always enjoyed taking in the aroma of the delicious Haitian cuisine filling the air. The smell of simmering garlic and onions always made me so happy to be reuniting with the family at the dinner table once again. The aroma of broiling meats in the oven made me want to burst into the kitchen to grab my share even before the cooking was done.

She always knew exactly how much salt to add or just the right amount of butter the recipe needed. She sliced potatoes and added a helping of cheese and knew the right amount of milk to added to the pot for the potatoes to cook and for the cheeses to melt.

Dinner time was one of the times that our family got to bond. It was an everyday thing but, nothing was better than sitting, laughing and enjoying the well-rounded meal of my mother's labors with people that loved me more than I could possibly love myself.

And then when the time would come and we were able to indulge into the elegantly adorned roasted turkey and stuffing, mashed potatoes, rice and bean sauce, nobody was willing to hesitate. The presentation of the dishes were always nice. My mom would make the food look pretty, just for us with garnishes on her meats and adding some type of décor to the food.

 As for me, I could not help but to have an insatiable hunger for more, because it was always so delicious and hearty and just everything a person could want that made dinner time the best time. Flavor simply burst into our mouths from a whisper to a scream. We couldn't help but to decorate smile onto our faces.

It was like an indulgent, family celebration every time we gathered together to enjoy a meal in harmony. Our family would sit, eat the warm morsels of the prepared foods while talk and burst out into gales of laughter at all the silly warmth people would add to the oasis of the dining room table. Dinner consisted of us spending a slice of time together with people we all revered. And so, eating and celebrating life together at the dinner table was always a stimulating experience.

Maybe one day I will get my skills together. They say that being obedient to a recipe equals success. I am more of a creative thinker and add my own ingredients not written on the actual pages of a cooking book. I am more of the type to look for new ideas and implement them based on me. My mom on the other hand is someone who made a meal and thought about every single person who would be present to sit at her dinner table and eat. Her meals were a genius body of work. She was like a Carol King to songs when it came to cooking. Even if she did not consume any of the food that she prepared, it was mostly to the desire of our hearts to make sure that we were satisfied with her selfless way of cooking things up in good faith. I only hope my scope of skills will be as good as hers someday. But based on her example of putting her foot into it, I know that one day I'll fly.